The Thoughts Of A "Sound Mind"

A Collection of Thoughts and Poems

Vanessa L. Graham

BookLeaf Publishing

India | USA | UK

Made with ❤ on the BookLeaf Publishing Platform
www.bookleafpub.in
www.bookleafpub.com

Dedication

To the kid whose voice was unheard and the thoughts
left unsaid.

Preface

*You owe reality nothing and the truth about your
feelings everything.*
— Richard Hugo

Acknowledgements

To the professors that never let up and pushed me forward when I wanted to step back.

The Library of You

Scars littered his body
like chapters in a novel.
Each holding its own story of him

Pages creased–
from years of rereading
Words smudged and illegible,
scatter the margins from years of rewriting

He– is the book I never want to stop reading.

No matter how well I know the stories,
each time I read, he gets a little bit clearer.

Each story,
each scar
I will continue to love and hold.

Enthused every time I get to bear witness
to its reading.

Running my hands down his spine,
feeling the well-worn surface from the amount my
hands have held him.

Flipping through the never-ending pages of our reality,
He is the book I'll never quite put down.

A Cemetery Sunset

The sound of the river was calming

As the sun began to set,
the world seemed to follow
quieting to a dull hum that surrounds us.

The rapids replaced the sounds of rushing cars
the silhouettes of trees danced
with a backdrop of cotton candy clouds.

There's a sense of comfort in the end of the day,
as well as the beauty –
of a new start...

If I could –
I would chase sunsets with you

I'd run toward the feeling of the world winding down,
the relief of a job well done
the warmth and safety of your side.

It is in that time,
that we are free from the obligations of life
and everything seems to slow as we gaze at the melting
pot above.

Maybe,
Just maybe –
within the ever-changing colors of our forever sky
we can find peace by slipping between the cracks
of rainbows
Freed from a world that demands monochromality

The Tapestry of Language

What is a word worth?
With phrases thrown around
like "actions speak louder than words"
or "a picture is worth a thousand...",
where do we draw the line of preference?

Images and sounds,
music and art alike,
crack
and carve
a way for unspoken emotions to be perceived.
Sometimes much better than words ever could.

At what point do we give them weight?
Yes,
we also have sayings such as
"the pen is mightier than the sword"
or the tales of how people "wrote their way into history".

For how long do words hold meaning?

Are they forever
like cobblestone roads
that hold up better than modern asphalt,
do they linger and fade
like dye on tongues,
or do they dissolve
instantaneously
like when cotton candy hits water?

Often words are thrown around,
repeated over and over each time
losing a little bit more of their meaning.

The repetition is relentless in its reconstruction–
the yeah's, the okay's and the I'm sorry's.
Sometimes–
even down to the I love you's.

Shadows

It's crazy looking back on the things I've written,
knowing what they came from
but feeling it's strength now.
The pain she felt,
incredibly real yet so distant now.
She was a boulder in a river
whilst I am a fallen leaf riding its current.

I envy her strength and passion.
She felt so strongly back then,
now only half-heartedly.
She stood tall as she was buried half beneath the soil.
Despite being stuck by everyone who told her she could
not,
she clawed for her freedom
disregarding all the damage it did.

You reap what you sow.
And that I do.
The damage is paid tenfold now.

No longer able to hold my ground.

Slouching has a new meaning now,
no longer referring to my posture
but the state in which my soul cowers
in the face of other people's thoughts.
A once extroverted child curls herself in the shadows
because it's easier not to be seen.

It's easier for your mind
to be passive when you don't like confrontation.
But your heart pays the toll.

I don't wish to go back to that time.
Living through it once
was more than enough.
I only wish to search the remains
and pick up the broken parts of me
that I've long since forgotten.

I want the confidence,
the reassurance,
the love I had not only for others but myself.
I want the sweet nothings of the dreams and aspirations
I once held so close to my heart.
The motivation that I could be whatever I wanted.

But these pieces are fragile.
They've already been shattered once
and are littered with cracks.
Some so deep,
that it's like they are clinging together as if their life
depended on it...

Maybe it does.

A Morning Vestige

Because you are not a
chalice
filled with sacred wine,
or the scooped hands
of far spent travelers,
your history is not that
of a great vessel.
You are not prestigiously posed
or displayed in glass cases
Often stacked
and pushed to the back of cupboards
You are not as decorative
as you are practical
But,
you are shapeless
and free.
You
are the essence of home;
of chilled days and hot drinks,
of sock clad feet and fireplace sitting

You

are the one I search for,

whether its for the memories you hold

or simply the way you feel

against the palm of my hand

A closeness to a part of me I can no longer reach out

and touch—

So when the chill sets in

and the rain taps on my window,

It is you,

I choose to spend my quiet time with

You

are the warmth savored—

in the fleeting moments of my life

The Silent Yearning

Colorless
the sky shifts into oblivion.
The sound of waves crashing
against unmoving boulders
is all but a gentle
hum.

Just feet beyond
the shore
the ocean lay a void.
Vast but not empty.

L'appel du vide

We crave its sanctum

Slumber's Sigh: A Lament for the Sleepless Moonlight

My vision grows hazy,
I find myself in a daze.
His arms cradle me,
his voice so sweetly laced with melancholy,
pleading for me to keep him company.

The exhaustion strangles me,
keeping me at bay as his tranquil lullaby soothes the
anxiety,
making everything seem fine.
The countless empty promises he's made of aiding me
through the harshness of
life,
vanishes when the golden glow looms on the horizon;
leaving me lifeless,
drained of all that remained.

Part of me yearns for his comforting embrace,
but knows all too well that it's pernicious.

The forever growing romance between a person and the
endless night,
like Cinderella at the ball but the clocks frozen at 11:59.
A dance of a lifetime.
Special.
Intoxicating.

So tonight, when he makes his way back to me,
I will greet him with open arms knowing that he is mine,
and mine alone.

My insomnia

Ode to Car Rides

The hum of tires
on freshly paved asphalt
ring clearer
than any chime
ever could

The music of
passing cars
and sidewalk chatter
create harmonies
unmatched.

The faint lull
of busy bodies
in a forever moving
town.

The paved paths
are never-ending,

as the maze
swallows its searchers.
Both dangerous
and calm.

Water lined trees
and winding back roads
are the only way
one can truly
relax.

Hot leather and cold leather
both sting the same
as it burns,
sticks,
and rips at the flesh
of its seater

City lights and stars
accompany the moon
as it lurks,
lays,
and tucks itself
into the reflection
of the lakes
and rivers

Open skies
and mounding fields
call to a
sanctity
only some
could imagine

Tears like tidal waves
that crash through
city walls,
laughs that break clouds
like sunlight
and roar like thunder,
snowflake smiles
and glossy eyes

The sheer awe
of freedom confined

Y Llegaron Las Flores (The Funeral)

Red
Red has never felt
so safe

In their ever-fleeting
ever-wilting
life

(Safe,
so safe)

Embraced by shadows
(smothered by shadows)
the branches creep,
the screams of leaves ring
In all the assumed misery
where else
can I call home
but the red

Nurture me,
Let me bloom
like the rose you are!
Let me grow sharp
with thorns of steel
Let me grow roots
that render me unmovable
Let me grow strong; enough
to withstand the harshest of winters

Let me...
let me...

To be like you
is to wilt gracefully
to be placed on coffins,
handed to lovers,
pinned to jackets and wrist bands,
to be suspended and preserved in death

(To be like you,
is to be red)

Time Capsule: We're Going to be Okay

"Time heals all wounds"

Some wounds never quite heal,
you just get used to their sting.
Tough love cost years of pain and self-pity.
Being that young,
you weren't ready
for the internal conflict to come.
Insecurities cast shadows
that need no light to be seen.
Ones that haunt into the night and linger in your soul.
Incandescent sobs
can't drown the fire
that blazes within the heart
of those trapped
by crude ideals.
It's so easy to feel lost to a sea of thoughts and
possibilities.
A craving for freedom but fear of the unknown

So wander

Wandering does not equate to lost,
but even if you are
that is okay too.
Even wide eyes can't see,
beyond the wall that occludes them

So wander
Let the veil drop.
Let the fire burn.
Let the waves crash.
Let the pain settle.
-V

Things I'm Afraid I'll Forget

What if I forget the laughs?
the lake days and park play sets,
the car rides and blaring music

those were my favorite

What if I forget my childhood home?
the chipped walls littered with photos,
the strip kitchen always too crowded,
the gold and burgundy walls of my parents bedroom

I wouldn't

What if I forget my father's hands?
the way they'd lift me to the sky,
the way they'd pick me up when I fell,
their safety and authority

how long has it been?

What if I forget the sibling love?
the fights, the tears, the makeups,
the homemade lightsabers and the fight scene
reenactments

I don't think I ever could

What if I forget my mother?
the way her lips brushed against my forehead on
sleepless nights,
the way her arms cradled me safe,
her unconditional love and faith

her sun-like smile

What if I forget myself?
The girl who laughed and played without a care,
the girl who didn't hold her tongue yet remained kind,
the girl who had big dreams and strove for them

that girl – she
she who listens to all except herself
she who carries too much of others, and all of her own
she who kills herself a little each day with fleeting
memories of the past

Am I allowed to forgive her?

Body

The long-planted seeds
Sown by your threads of shame
Steeped in the soil, that is my soul
Ingrained fat shames burned into the most inner layers
of my being,
How dare you sit there and tell me how to wear my skin,
Whether it's something to be proud of,
or not.
This body has been pinched and pulled, broken and beat.
It's been a battle ground rather than a safe zone,
A weapon of self-destruction,
and I will NOT hate this body anymore.
This body is mine
and this body is beautiful,
It was not made for you to pick apart.
It was not made to make you feel comfortable.
My body is more faithful than you will EVER be
Through the skipped meals, insomnia and all
It's been faithful,
It's about time I returned the favor,

This body is mine
and this body is beautiful,
It's worth holding onto.
I know that now.

At What Cost

At what cost is a human life?
The "dire" needs of a nation
drown the cries of millions

Where we preach of seeds sown
on stolen grounds and blazing fires
And for what?
the "publics" desires?

At what point do deaf ears ring?
Not yet,
when murder sits on our porch step
and knocks at our door

When children's lives
weigh less than law
and fingers point anywhere but—

At what point do the tears of mothers
flood the dams of capital walls

and wash away the blood

To whom do we owe the pleasure
To whom do we thank for our safety
or lack thereof—

When fear surrounds our daily lives,
is there really a chance to be free
in a nation that claims such ideals...

I Refuse

I refuse to be a shadow
dancing in the background
of this life
I refuse to be the misguided love
of your self satisfaction and hate
I refuse to be the hindrance
that stops dreams
from coming true
I refused to be the villain in your story
just because you want me to

I return to you the deceptions,
the years of gas lighting
and "trying to make this work"
I return the self signed script
of the lies I knew weren't true,
I return the hate
that boils only in your presence
—still

I return to myself
the love and selflessness that I showed
whilst trying to pick up your broken pieces
(I never had glue strong enough and you liked to
fall)

I take back the control you had over my life.

Torch Song

She,
is a fire
lit in the rushing tides
of a deep ocean
where only she
and her thoughts
exist

Her very being
burns her alive
She boils
until her conscience
is evaporated
and still

She,
has no ownership
of her lips
Only in the existence
of stage lights

does her fire burn
freely *(without internal destruction)*

Only there,
does she truly glow
Powered by emotions
long sealed
and festering

Only there,
does she find
freedom.

Don't Play with Fire

My mind is lost
But my heart's awake
I can hear it in my ears, as it screams in pain.
Broken in pieces and cast aside,
In a dark, damp alley is where it resides.
Thrown under tires so many times before,
"These tracks weren't there" I swore.
Peace and tranquility so long forgotten,
Only ever present when the sky has fallen.
But only in the literal sense of a city gone dark.
My thoughts start racing, only starting to spark.
A lit candle in a dark abandoned house,
The flickering flame only visible to a mouse.
One small gust and the flame dies quick,
But one small push and the flames stick.
A small abandoned house now burnt to the ground,
All because of a flame that refused to drown.
It's soft and delicate yet lethal and strict
The choice is yours, which do you pick?
Your mind may say one thing, and your heart another.

But which flame is which is something you have to
discover.
So, proceed with caution and listen to what's been said,
Because when you play with fire you might just end up
dead.

In a Box Under my Bed

In a box under my bed...
lay the zombies of my past
not quite dead,
not quite alive

The past versions of me
some soft,
some social,
some angry,
some scared.

All lost
and yet to be found.

The disconnect of what was
and what can never be
trapped in the "what if"
terrified of the "what can"
never truly here.

The only thing *claiming*
this existence
are the printed memories of me.

In that box lies
dreams and ambitions.
Years of practiced patience
and passive smiles.
A kindness and hunger
for a wanting
future.

A Map

Home; east of childhood
sadness and
west of childhood wonder.
The city center not too far
woods minutes away
beautiful yet mundane
Home; far from where I am
across vast oceans
rolling hills and open skies
self love replacing
self depreciation
North of love
South of happiness–
true contentment

What I remember without qualification is her.

Her smiles
her energy,
the love she had for others and herself.

\----------------------------------

I remember the dancing and laughter from family parties
She was a firecracker
you didn't know was lit
Dancing around the tables
flipping her hair
Her family calling out,
"She's a wild girl" with laughter in their throats
But she paid them no mind,
"I like wild"

\------------------------------

I remember our family albums,
there wasn't a day when some crazy thing I did as a
child,
wasn't mentioned.
A visual footprint of the parts of me I had forgotten–

parts I lived through but didn't know.
Our family homes' ring with the laughter
of family jokes
stemming from childish actions
and unfiltered answers
I wonder,
at what point did it become a blockade?
A split from who I was–
I know I used to be the girl in those family photos
The one they love to recall...
But I can't help but wonder if she is still me,
and if not, what happened?

I remember the concerts and the recordings after–
The girl in the video seems like a stranger now,
there she stood a girl blowing kisses to the audience
excited and eager to be seen.
She stuck out with her wide eyes and smiling face.
In that moment,
she was undeniably happy where she was
and with the show she had just put on
you could tell
she was right where she needed to be.

I remember is the dance studio
my reflection in the mirror
she too is stranger

She stood tall,
confident–
shoulders back with her head held high,
she knew her part and she could play it well
A leader,
She was acknowledged
for her skills and dedication.
Something she always wanted.

Time and time again,
I saw this girl–
she was right, smart and well loved,
She was a kind girl overflowing with love for other
people.
I wonder where she would be if she had stayed the
same?

Love is a Fickle Thing

Lonely.
Lonely like the blooming harvest moon.
Shrouded in a haze of mist,
Not entirely alone,
But just enough.
As the wind picks up,
Casting the clouds astray,
The stars dance across the unseen horizon.
The people down below praise,
For the moon is no longer lonely.
The moon gazes at the stars,
Yearning for their friendship.
This,
This is a different type of lonely.
The longing for something platonic,
A companion to confide in.
The moon longs for them,
Though he knows they're unreachable.
Light years away, yet he cries for them.
His voice muted by the space.

Entranced by their light,
He craves them.
To have something worth admiring.
He was blinded by them.
Focusing solely on their light,
That he failed to recognize,
The love he received from the ground below.
People gaze at him as he does the stars.
Thankful for every night,
He comes out to play.

How Could I Ever Say the Words

I hold so many secrets in my heart
that I feel like I could burst any second
I hold many fears in my heart
But the thing I fear most–
is that if I were to open myself
and hand you my pain,
you wouldn't recognize the person standing
in front of you.
A person that you loved
would be a stranger.
That you would deny
the person that I am
for the image that you thought I was.
I'm so afraid of that rejection.
that you wouldn't want to learn
to love the scars that scatter both my body and heart.
That you'd rather push away the idea of my pain
then try to love it.
The damaged left scars

so deep
that I can't bear to look
at how they've healed.
I can't fathom how they've decided
to mend themselves.
I fear that you wouldn't want to know
the stories behind my heart,
and brush it off as if they weren't there.
For this reason,
I don't know if I will ever bear myself to you